T0341478

blasts cries laughter

NEW DIRECTIONS POETRY PAMPHLETS

lawrence ferlinghetti

BLASTS
CRIES
LAUGHTER

NEW DIRECTIONS POETRY PAMPHLET #9

Copyright © 1988, 1998, 2002, 2014 by Lawrence Ferlinghetti

All rights reserved. Except for brief passages quoted in a newspaper, magazine, radio, television, or website review, no part of this book may be reproduced in any form or by any means, electronic or mechanical, including photocopying and recording, or by any information storage and retrieval system, without permission in writing from the Publisher.

Cover design by Office of Paul Sahre
Interior design by Erik Rieselbach
Manufactured in the United States of America
New Directions Books are printed on acid-free paper.
First published as New Directions Poetry Pamphlet #9 in 2014

Library of Congress Cataloging-in-Publication Data
Ferlinghetti, Lawrence.
[Poems. Selections]
Blasts, cries, laughter / Lawrence Ferlinghetti.
pages cm. — (New Directions poetry pamphlet ; #9)
ISBN 978-0-8112-2178-8 (alk. paper)
I. Title.
PS3511.E557B53 2014
811'.54—dc23   2013030595

10 9 8 7 6 5 4 3 2

New Directions Books are published for James Laughlin
by New Directions Publishing Corporation
80 Eighth Avenue, New York, NY 10011

*"When you are up to your neck in merde,
there's nothing to do but sing."*
—*Samuel Beckett*

THE LORD'S LAST PRAYER

Our father whose art's in heaven
Hollow be thy name
Unless things change
Thy kingdom come and gone
Thy will will be undone
On earth as it isn't heaven
Give us this day our daily bread
At least three times a day
And lead us not into temptation
too often on weekdays
But deliver us from evil
Whose presence remains unexplained
In thy kingdom of power and glory
Ah, Man!

CUT DOWN!

Cut down Cut down Cut down
Cut down your grass roots and too-wild weeds
Cut down cut down those wild sprouts
your too-wild buds your too-wild shoots
Cut down your upstart vines and voices
your hardy volunteers and pioneers
Cut down cut down your alien corn
Cut down your crazy introverts
tongue-tied lovers of the subjective
Pull down your vanity, man, pull down
the wild ones the wild spirits the crazy bastards
far-out weirdos and spaced-out rappers
stoned-out visionaries and peacenik pinkies
Have-nots and Occupiers in tent cities
desert rats and monkey wrenchers
Easy Riders Midnight Cowboys
and dreamers in narco nirvanas
soapbox agitators and curbstone philosophers
Cut down cut down all your alienated loners
spaced-out freaks and too free thinkers
wide-eyed poets with too wild minds
self-exiled in their own land
O smelting-pot America!

BLIND POET

Performed with a blindfold and a cane

I am a blind poet
I am your blind poet and painter
full of fantastic phrases and images
I am painting the landscape of my bent soul
and the soul of mankind
as I see it
I am giving it a voice
I am singing folk songs
about the downtrodden masses
and the rich on their fat asses
I am the painter who feels
with his fingers
I am the blind seeing-eye poet
I see what you can't see
I eat well and drink well
and dream of great epics
I am your postmodern pastmodern
multimedia artist
I am the most avant of the avant
I'm site-specific and totally conceptual
Even the greatest critics have been baffled
by my profundity
I once knew Andy Warhol
And I've slept with you know whom

And I'm a fast-speaking man
your deconstructed language poet
your far-out poet
full of ecstasies and visions
your wandering workshop poet
your hairy university poet
with tenure
your buddhist quietest poet
I go on poetry reading tours
where everything is paid for
I hear everything
and it's grist to my mill
I use it all
to make great sound poetry
or great concrete poetry
that no one can see through
Life is a real dream
and I am dreaming it
And I've got it all in my head
the Song of Humanity
and the Song of Inhumanity
I'll paint you a profound picture
an action painting
a gestural painting
nothing but pure gesture
I'll write you a far-out song
of common people
If I take off my mask
I'll see the real world

for the first time
But I won't take it off
It fits too well
It's a perfect fit
It's too comfortable
And I've got my career to think of
my life to think of
We only live once
and living *very* well is the best revenge
Get your own blindfold
You can't have mine
You'll have to face the world without it
And anyway I'm too young to die
I'm an American
and Americans don't *die*
We're the conquerors
We're the new roman emperors
We're conquering the world
It's the invisible empire
of genial vulture capitalism
And democracy *is* capitalism
No more poor people
No more starving and dying
No more huddled masses in our empire
The rising tide lifts all boats
If you've got a boat

A CASINO CULTURE

It's Autogeddon
An Armageddon of autos
In the City of Angels
In downtown Denver
In Chicago and Manhattan
Mexico City and Milan
Calcutta and Tokyo
Drowned in the bad breath of machines
The sun's wearing shades
The ozone layer coughing smog
The ecosystem as finely balanced as a mobile
A computer about to crash

A casino culture out of control
A hole in its ozone soul
A sweepstakes Winner Take All
A shooting gallery for masters of war
A bull market with toreadors
A runaway juggernaut heading for naught
A runaway robot bombing through cities
The hydraulic brakes blown
And no one can slow it down
Not even the UN not even the EU
Not even the Pope or you name it

America America
oh beautiful with spacious skies

In Las Vegas they've made
a replica of it—the whole tamale—the whole shebang—
The Eiffel Tower
The Statue of Liberty
The George Washington Bridge
The Golden Gate
King Kong and the Empire State

"Swept with con
the millions stand under the signs"
Internet gamblers and dot-com billionaires
Coked up in stretch limos
Everybody playing the slots
The predatory ladies purr
The pinballs whirr

The whole spinning world lights up
TILT!
A billion jackpots blow with a bang
"Kingfishers catch fire
Dragonflies draw flame"
Shoppers carried by escalators
into the flames
Skin-deep civilization
gone in a flash of samsara

Rockabye baby!

Swing low sweet chariot

HISTORY OF THE AIRPLANE

(Music: U.S. National Anthem at half speed)

And the Wright brothers said they thought they had invented
something that could make peace on earth (if the wrong
brothers didn't get hold of it) when their wonderful flying
machine took off at Kitty Hawk into the kingdom of birds
but the parliament of birds was freaked out by this man-
made bird and fled to heaven

And then the famous Spirit of Saint Louis took off eastward
and flew across the Big Pond with Lindy at the controls in his
leather helmet and goggles hoping to sight the doves of peace
but he did not Even though he circled Versailles

And then the famous Yankee Clipper took off in the opposite
direction and flew across the terrific Pacific but the pacific
doves were frightened by this strange amphibious bird and
hid in the orient sky

And then the famous Flying Fortress took off bristling with
guns and testosterone to make the world safe for peace and
capitalism but the birds of peace were nowhere to be found
before or after Hiroshima

And so then clever men built bigger and faster flying machines and these great man-made birds with jet plumage flew higher than any real birds and seemed about to fly into the sun and melt their wings and like Icarus crash to earth

And the Wright brothers were long forgotten in the high-flying bombers that now began to visit their blessings on various Third Worlds all the while claiming they were searching for doves of peace

And they kept flying and flying until they flew right into the 21st century and then one fine day a Third World struck back and stormed the great planes and flew them straight into the beating heart of Skyscraper America where there were no aviaries and no parliaments of doves and in a blinding flash America became a part of the scorched earth of the world

And a wind of ashes blows across the land
And for one long moment in eternity
There is chaos and despair
And buried loves and voices
Cries and whispers
Fill the air
Everywhere

FROM THE GREENPEACE DREAMBOOK

Aboard the S.S. James Bay, October 4, 1977

Dreamt of
    Moby Dick the Great White Whale
    cruising about with a sign on him—
    "I am what is left of Wild Nature"
 And Ahab pursuing in a jet boat
    with ray guns and jet harpoons
    and super depth charges
    and napalm flamethrowers and
    electric underwater vibrators
    and the whole gory glorious efficient
    military-political-industrial-scientific
    technology of the greatest civilization
    mother earth has ever known
    devoted to the absolute extinction
    of the natural world
And Captain Ahab
    Captain Death
        Captain Apocalypse at the helm
                of the killer ship of death
And the blue-eyed whales
             exhausted and running
      but still
           singing to each other ...

CRIES OF ANIMALS DYING

In a dream within a dream I dreamt a dream
of all the animals dying out
all animals everywhere
dying & dying
the wild animals the long-haired animals
winged animals feathered animals
clawed & scaled & furry animals
rutting & dying & dying
in shrinking rainforests
in piney woods and high sierras
on shrinking prairies & tumbleweed mesas
captured beaten starved & stunned
cornered and traded
species not meant to be nomadic
wandering rootless as man
All the animals crying out
in their hidden places
slinking away and crawling away
through the last wild places
through the dense underbrush
the last Great Thickets
beyond the mountains
crisscrossed with switchbacks
beyond the marshes
beyond the plains and fences
(the West won with barbed-wire machines)

in the high country
in the low country
in the bayous
crisscrossed with highways

In a dream within a dream I dreamt
of how they feed & rut & run & hide
how the seals are beaten on ice fields
the soft white furry seals with eggshell skulls
the great green turtles beaten & eaten
exotic birds netted & caged & tethered
rare wild beasts & strange reptiles & weird woozoos
hunted down for zoos
by bearded black marketers
who afterwards ride around Singapore
in German limousines
with French whores

In a dream within a dream I dreamt a dream
of all the earth drying up
to a burnt cinder
in the famous Greenhouse Effect
under a canopy of carbon dioxide
breathed out by a billion
infernal combustion engines
mixed with the sweet smell of burning flesh
And all the animals calling to each other
In codes we never understand
The seal and steer cry out

in the same voice the same cry
The wounds never heal
in the commonweal of animals
We steal their lives
to feed our own
and with their lives
our dreams are sown

In a dream within a dream I dreamt a dream
of the daily scrimmage for existence
in the wind-up model of the universe
the spinning meat-wheel world
about to consume itself

SHOW YOUR SON . . .

So show your son a sunset
                before they're all gone
        advised an old Lefty
            exhibiting the usual paranoia
                      of the Left
      that has now spilled over
              on ecologists
          and others of their ilk
always ranting about the ozone hole
    and cancer and smoking
       and the population of the world
                  doubling again
           by the year two thousand twenty
and about how the earth
           is coming to a sudden bad end

Whereas we all know the media and
      the oil combines and
       the tobacco companies and
           the industry scientists and
     the industrial perplex in general
        are all telling us the whole bull
         and nothing but the bull
So no need to worry
      "No problem"
           as they say downtown

Even if those clouds out the window
                              look a bit strange
And the droughts all over the world
            aren't really all that bad
                  because it can't happen here
                              as they used to say in the Thirties
And all those jet streams from airlines
                  really don't spew more
                        cancerous exhaust
                              than a billion cars

And those aren't really
                        Sun Dogs in the too-brilliant sun
And sunsets are still sunsets
            even if they are only
                              one-color sunsets
      over which pilots are reporting
                  clouds are lower than they used to be
                              before the Greenhouse years
Whereas sunsets now are more like "heart events"
            with pollution like bad cholesterol
                  jamming the arteries of the universe
                  and obstructing circulation
                  and causing systemic disasters

And our evening spread across the sky
                  like a patient passed out upon a table

MAHLER'S APOCALYPSE

At the Michael Tilson Thomas concert
The big brass all of a sudden catches fire
With timpani crashing
And flames shooting out of silver horns
And drums beating at the flames
Ands violins violently fanning them
Mit größter Vehemenz

And Mahler's flagship foundering
in twenty-first-century seas
With the conductor at the helm
going down with it—
Like mad Artaud
signaling through the flames!

PITY THE NATION

(After Khalil Gibran)

Pity the nation whose people are sheep
and whose shepherds mislead them
Pity the nation whose leaders are liars
Whose sages are silenced
and whose bigots haunt the airwaves
Pity the nation that raises not its voice
but aims to rule the world
by force and by torture
And knows
no other language but its own
Pity the nation whose breath is money
and sleeps the sleep of the too well fed
Pity the nation Oh pity the people of my country
My country, tears of thee
Sweet land of liberty!

SOUTH OF THE BORDER

Gringos and gringas in beach chairs
        slurping down the margaritas
    and listening to the mariachis
          and their thumping guitarrones
And never ever hearing
    the distant drums of the dispossessed
        where promises made in the plazas
           are betrayed in the back country

DRAGON'S TEETH

A headless man is running
down the street
He is carrying his head
in his hands
A woman runs after him
She has his heart
in her hands
And the drones keep coming
And those people keep running
down the dirt streets
Not the same two people
but thousands of others & brothers
All running from the drones
sowing pure hate
and for every drone that zeroes in
on these running people
up spring a thousand Bin Ladens
a thousand new terrorists
Like dragon's teeth sown
From which armed warriors spring up
Crying for blood & revenge

SONG OF THE THIRD WORLD BIRDS

A cock cried out in my sleep
       somewhere in Middle America
              to awake the Middle Mind of America
And the cock cried out
       to awake me to see
          a sea of birds
              flying over me
                   across America

And there were birds of every color
      black birds & brown birds
         & yellow birds & red birds
           from the lands of every
              liberation movement

And all these birds circled the earth
     and flew over every great nation
         and over Fortress America
            with its great Eagle and its thunderbolts

And all the birds cried out with one voice
    the voice of those who have no voice
    the voice of the invisibles of the world
  the voice of the dispossessed of the world
      the fellaheen peoples of earth
      who are now all rising up

And which side are you on
         sang the birds
   Oh which side are you on
       Oh which side are you on
   in the Third World War
         the War with the Third World?

WHO ARE THE BARBARIANS?

I am the Greek senator
waiting for the barbarians
to relieve us of our destinies
and solve all our problems

But who *are* the barbarians?
Are they the avid macho fans
screaming for blood
at kickboxing matches
or the pretty boys and girls
glued to computers and cell phones
or the short-haired gents in suits
in downtown skyscrapers
or the hungry ones at our borders?

Brother, look no further
We are the ones our fathers warned us about
the enlightened ones
born to rule the world
through computers that ensure
total isolation and loneliness
Don't call me I'll call you
No need for conversation anymore
A casual cynicism is fashionable
and the Twitterati rule

A great sleep
has overtaken everyone
at our handheld machines

The violins of autumn
are heard through the trees
while the white horses of the sea
still dash upon our sands
with a great lost roaring

TO THE ORACLE AT DELPHI

Read by the author to the Oracle at Delphi,
Unesco World Poetry Day, 3/21/01

Great Oracle, why are you staring at me,
do I baffle you, do I make you despair?
I, Americus, the American,
wrought from the dark in my mother long ago,
from the dark of ancient Europa—
Why are you staring at me now
in the dusk of our civilization—
Why are you staring at me
as if I were America itself
the new Empire
far greater than any in ancient days
with its electronic highways
carrying its corporate monoculture
around the world
And English the Latin of our day—

Great Oracle, sleeping through the centuries,
Awaken now at last
And tell us how to save us from ourselves
and how to survive our own rulers
who have made a plutocracy of our democracy
in the Great Divide
between the rich and the poor
in whom Walt Whitman heard America singing

O long-silent Sybil,
You of the winged dreams,
Speak out from your temple of light
as the serious constellations
with Greek names
still stare down on us
as a lighthouse moves its megaphone
over the sea
Speak out and shine upon us
the sea-light of Greece
the diamond light of Greece

Farseeing Sybil, forever hidden,
Come out of your cave at last
And speak to us in the poet's voice
the voice of the fourth person singular
the voice of the inscrutable future
the voice of the people mixed
with a wild soft laughter—
And give us new dreams to dream,
new myths to live by!

ORACULAR VISIONS

Athens 3/22/01

The isles of Greece
          the isles of Greece!
The Delphic mysteries
            the Golden Fleece
The light upon the sea
                eternal
The horses of Achilles
         weeping for Achilles
The loves of Sappho
             in the night
The songs and cries of Sappho
The Delphic prophecies
The Elysian mysteries
The sound of revelry by night
         on Mount Olympus
The orgasmic cries
           of Dionysus
The high breasts of Helen
The long fair hair
        of Helen
Her darkened eyes
The longing eyes of Penelope
         Aie! Aie! Ulysses!
And Audiart Audiart
   where thy bodice laces part

And then the cawing of crows
Mixed with the cry
                    of nightingales
          at the Fountain of Castallia
And then the anger of the gods
And then the dire prophecies
The wailing of sibyls and sirens
The cries of the vestal virgins
The cries of Icarus
                    falling from the sky
The foundering
                    of ships at sea
The cries of the blinded Cyclops
                         in his cave
And the sun the setting sun
                    over the isles of Greece
The sound of axes
                         in the wood
                    in the sacred grove
And the Golden Bough unfound
                              beyond us still
The dancers gone
                    under the hill

Ah let the Golden Age return
Before all ages end
And we must burn!

THE FIRST AND THE LAST
OF EVERYTHING

The first fine dawn of life on earth
The first cry of man in the first light
The first firefly flickering at night
The first song of love and forty cries of despair
The first voyage of Vikings westward
The first sighting of the New World
           from the crow's nest of a Spanish galleon
The first Pale Face meeting the first native American
The first Dutch trader in Mannahatta
The first settler on the first frontier
The first Home Sweet Home so dear
The first wagon train westward
The first sighting of the Pacific by Lewis & Clark
The first cry of "Mark, twain!" on the Mississippi
The first desegregation by Huck & Jim on a raft at night
The first Buffalo nickel and the last buffalo
The first barbed-wire fence and the last of the open range
The last cowboy on the last frontier
The first skyscraper in America
The first home run hit at Yankee Stadium
The first ballpark hotdog with mustard
The last War To End All Wars
The last Wobbly and the last Catholic Anarchist
The last living member of the Abraham Lincoln Brigade

The last bohemian in a beret
The last homespun politician and the first stolen election
The first plane to hit the first Twin Tower
The birth of a vast national paranoia
The first President to become an international criminal
        for crimes against humanity
                making America a terrorist state
The dark dawn of American corporate fascism
The next-to-last free speech radio
The next-to-last independent newspaper raising hell
The next-to-last independent bookstore with a mind of its own
The next-to-last lefty looking for Obama Nirvana
The first fine day of the Wall Street Occupation
                to set forth upon this continent a new nation!

MAGIC THEATER

Sitting on a bench at the Ferry Building San Francisco
on the last frontier in the land of the free
facing the sea I see
a young stud arrive and sit
on the bench next to me
He has a croissant in a paper bag and
he has coffee in a paper cup and
he proceeds to drink coffee and
eat the croissant while
all the while looking seaward
but he sees nothing but his life
spread out before him on
the laughing waves and
in the meantime the ferry arrives
and disgorges its morning cargo
into the City yes
the City that hold so much promise
with its white buildings rising up and up
O radiant city
where now the guy gets up and
disappears into this city and
after a while a comely woman
A young woman
Une jeune fille en fleur
comes and sits on the same bench
just vacated by the young stud and

after a while another man appears and
sits down next to her on the little bench as
she continues crying and
he says nothing as
some Persian pigeons strut about on the
hard dock and one of them comes over and
cocks his head at the woman and the man
And despair and desire are seated on a bench
where after a while
the man tries to speak to her but
the words catch in his throat and
he falls silent as
she continues weeping and
after a while he gets up and
looks at her and walks away
without looking back as
she continues weeping as
the pigeon also walks away and
after a while the ferry departs
with a very few escaping passengers and
the sun shines down and
after a while the woman gets up and
walks away without looking back
leaving the handkerchief with her tears
on the bench in the sun and
after a while
a man with a bag and a pointed stick
spears the handkerchief and
shakes it loose into his bag as

the sun continues shining
on the empty bench while
another ferry arrives and
disgorges its humans and
another man and another woman arrive
and occupy the bench in the sun and
look longing into each other's eyes
as the sun shines down on them
in the morning of their lives

Ah sweet the mornings
when the sun shines on love

EXTASIS

Ecstasy and its fellows
or its virgins
(some of them Extra Virgin)
is only for the very young
or the very old
who are so bold as to think
ecstasy ought to be
the aim of the life of the free
as for instance
when we stand dumbstruck
before the late sun slanting
through the trees
the ground of a sudden streaked
with bright shadows
born of eternity
and the ochre paint of the last light
pouring over us

Aye let us like moths fly straight into it
and burn up in a bright flare
in the final extasis!

"EYES, DREAMS, LIPS, AND THE NIGHT GOES..."

—Ezra Pound, "Italian Campagna"

Eyes, dreams, lips—
  and words ensnare them
     if we bare them
        to mind's merciless lingua
What else to say
       to do
         but sing
           Aie! Aie!
And let pure ecstasy be king

TRAGICOMEDY

The classical masks of
                    tragedy and comedy
            superimposed
                    upon each other
                through which the poet speaks
            simultaneously
                sometimes break out
                            rhapsodically
                    in riotous
                        uncontrollable laughter
        So that naturally
                the most Absurd
                        tragicomedies
                                follow after

KEENING

(for Philip Lamantia)

But what is that laughter under the hill

It's the laughter of the Marvelous
> of the Invisible
>> of the Absurd

Since there isn't any longer any Away
>   (On the island furthest out
>>   there's a Club Med)
>>>   we seek the island inside us
>>   an island in the sun
>>>   a wild calypso place
>>>>   an isle of last escape
>>   the land that is unconquerable
>>>   that cannot be consumed

There is a passionate yearning
>   a longing for wildness
>>   a love of wildness
>>   at the heart of every history

From Caliban to Gauguin
>   From Rousseau's noble savage
>>   to Rimbaud's Drunken Boat
>>>   and Whitman's first barbaric yawp

From the Roanoke colonists
        (who disappeared into the wilderness
          leaving a note behind:
              "Gone to Croatan")
    to London's Call of the Wild
      to Kerouac's Cassady
        whose hot rod was his horse
   and Ken Kesey in his bus
    with signs reading "Further"
It is the land of heretics and witches
     runaway slaves and mountain men
        Burning Men and *poètes maudits*

We hear their high laughter
    We hear their high keening
      like the tight light at the end of a tunnel!

WITH BECKETT

I dreamt I saw Samuel Beckett last night
walking through the little park
behind the dark brooding hulk
of the cathedral of Notre Dame
where the leaves of the *marronniers*
quivered in the rain
He was wearing a worn tweed coat
with collar turned up
And I imagined he had just come
from the Théâtre de la Poche
where they had just played in French
the thousandth performance of "Waiting for Godot"
And he sat down on a wet bench
and pretended to cry as he laughed
and pretended to laugh as he cried

And I was with him sitting there
under the chestnut trees
mon semblable mon frère!